# REALTY HIGHWAY

*The Drive for Real Estate Industry Evolution*

J. Michael Nolen Jr.

Copyright © 2015 J. Michael Nolen Jr.
All rights reserved.

ISBN: 1503146049
ISBN 13: 9781503146044

# Contents

| | |
|---|---:|
| Chapter One: How's Real Estate? | 1 |
| Chapter Two: Outreach | 5 |
| Chapter Three: My World | 8 |
| Chapter Four: Perspectives | 12 |
| Chapter Five: Preferences | 22 |
| Chapter Six: Ignorance | 27 |
| Chapter Seven: Information | 30 |
| Chapter Eight: Stats | 36 |
| Chapter Nine: Transaction-Centered | 38 |
| Chapter Ten: Directories | 40 |
| Chapter Eleven: Searches | 41 |
| Chapter Twelve: Purchases | 48 |
| Chapter Thirteen: Possibilities | 49 |
| Chapter Fourteen: Alternatives | 51 |
| Chapter Fifteen: What's Next? | 53 |
| Resources | 59 |

# I
# How's Real Estate?

Who doesn't ask a Realtor® "How's real estate?" Most aren't looking for a long dissertation, yet in today's market, a flippant answer isn't enough. And a response like "Across the nation, local markets vary greatly" doesn't begin to tell the story of the wide disparity in local real estate markets, especially since the market crash of 2008.

Fortunately, though, an abundance of data is collected and analyzed on each and every diverse local market. Such information is publicly available, but not widely distributed. Perhaps this is because, traditionally, a buyer simply hires a real estate professional and follows his or her guidance. When buyers do this, they need only a cursory knowledge of real estate. The real estate professional's service is only sought for a finite period of time, notably when someone is considering renting, buying, selling, or exchanging real estate. The rest of the time, the public mostly remains disengaged. Oh, there is plenty of generalized talk about real estate, but analysis of data and real estate news that specifically relates to homeowners' property or to planned purchases is rare.

By 2008, when the bottom fell out of real estate prices, it became apparent that this formula needed updating. The ripple effects of the crash were felt everywhere, by holders of real estate and by those not in the market, by those who were highly leveraged in real estate and by those who were not. Given the severity of the recession, the situation going forward cries out for change in the way real estate is transacted.

Such changes should entail a public that is more informed about real estate, where virtually everyone has some basic level of pertinent knowledge. Where direct access to real estate-related data and the tools necessary to analyze such data in order to make better real estate decisions, is the norm.

I'm truly shocked that a public that demands innovation (or at least an app) for everything is content to allow real estate professionals to essentially determine what information they receive and when they receive it. After all, the real estate professional's data source is the vendors they hire to analyze homeowner real estate transactions. It's the homeowners' data. Homeowners should be granted reasonable access to it. Most homeowners have no idea of the amount and type of information available to real estate professionals, and few Realtors® use the data adequately to ensure the interests of homeowners.

So, in short, the data should be better distributed. But is that the only change needed in the real estate industry? What about the act of a homeowner "listing" property with a real estate professional on the Multiple Listing Service? Certainly hiring a real estate professional is advisable, but alternatives will be expanded with new and improved real estate website services.

Can you visualize the general public, pulling up a dashboard of sorts on their computer screens, and finding real estate information that pertains directly to them, neatly placed, with tools for analyzing it at their disposal? It might automatically track the equity in the real estate they own and include a form to complete for placing their property on the market and a space to receive instantly the assistance of a trained real estate professional.

In this little book, I build a case for an innovative, interactive real estate platform to increase public awareness and knowledge of the real estate market. I recognize recent real estate industry progress and encourage a more cohesive effort going forward. Primarily, though, I'm looking to give voice to those who have been hurt by the downturn in real estate prices and to spur a conversation leading to real help for the homeowner. Help, that comes by way of innovation.

Herein, we will explore the trends and innovations that are leading us in that direction, as well as the reasons the movement is so slow in developing. Additionally, we review the real estate market of today, with tips for real estate professionals, individual homeowners, and future homeowners, in navigating a real estate market much unlike that of our forefathers.

Perhaps, instead of the public asking the real estate professional, "How's real estate?" the real estate professional should inquire of the property owner, "How's *your* real estate?" Finally, once the public is provided with more access to real estate data, the real question to the homeowner should be as follows: "How did you make use of the abundance of pertinent real estate data made available to you?"

Realtors® should take courage and not fear showering the public with information. We need fewer gatekeepers and more librarians; less control and more order. Let the public feel the weight of this responsibility.

The title of this book, *Realty Highway*, was inspired by Wall Street, and the fact that the real estate sector has suffered greatly since the meltdown of real estate prices. Figuratively speaking, if the financial markets have a street, it will take a highway for real estate to regain its once-elevated status among market sectors. The National Association of Realtors (NAR) states that "the survival and growth of free institutions and of our civilization relies" on a strong real estate market. That said, the tools of the real estate industry—platforms, dashboards, apps, and so forth—must be formidable and readily available to the public. For purposes of this publication, the name given to the various real estate-related platforms, dashboards, and apps, both present and proposed, is Realty Highway. It's a path forward for real estate transactions, a way to approach the future, both for the public and the real estate professional.

Out of the shambles of crisis, real estate and financial professionals have an opportunity to take a leading role in returning the real estate market to its former status. If they don't act, they're leaving the future of the industry to the whims of whoever does take the lead in the real estate market.

Most importantly, the public needs to be involved in the real estate market recovery. To do that, they need resources and instruction on how to use the information and tools available to them. That is where leadership should be involved.

# II

# Outreach

Welcome to the trenches of a real estate war zone. No, this isn't a military exercise or a discussion of real estate sales tactics. Rather, I'm inviting you to view the economy through my weathered eyes and to see, at ground level, the impact that the real estate meltdown has had on the lives of those living at its epicenter: Polk County, Florida. It's been about eight years now since the bust in the real estate market, and yet the headline of today's local newspaper reads: "Polk Leads US in Underwater Homes."

Polk County is a large, mostly rural area (roughly 80 percent the size of Delaware) and the home of the Lakeland/Winter Haven metropolitan statistical area (MSA). But mostly it's the bedroom community for both the Tampa and Orlando metro areas. Observations and lessons learned from what occurred here should stimulate discussion, and at least partially, explain why our nation's economy is not expanding at a faster pace.

Today, the news and views expressed by the media mostly come from those with a perspective skewed by the grandeur of Silicon Valley, Big Oil, Big Government, Wall Street, or Hollywood. As they report on national stats, the commentators seemingly imply, "We're doing so well! What's the matter with the rest of you?" But what they are truly asking is, "What is creating this headwind that is keeping the entire US economy from experiencing the growth of the stock market?"

Of course, low wages are often spoken of as the culprit, and naturally, that's a concern. However, the anemic real estate market is the underlying problem. Homeowners' outlooks for the future brighten as the equity in their property grows. Equity in real estate supports spending, impacts job growth, and improves wages.

This glimpse into my world provides context for ongoing trends—trends that expose problems within the traditional real estate market. It also indicates the grave importance of correcting the issues soon and draws attention to what individuals can do to protect themselves from real estate downturns.

However, this book is not meant to be an intensely detailed how-to manual. Instead, it represents a discussion of basic real estate principles and an outreach to the public, to Silicon Valley and the data scientists who work there, and to the real estate-related community of businesses and associations, in the spirit of entrepreneurism and the free market. It encourages open-minded discussions about the future of the real estate industry.

*Realty Highway* is a plea for a quick, open-market solution to the problems enumerated within, realizing that areas like the one where I live and work (the last to recover from the recession) will probably be the first to return to recession when interest rates rise significantly or the next calamity occurs.

Ultimately, long-term solutions to our nation's and her citizenry's financial problems will come as the consumer is better informed and participating in a user-friendly real estate market.

But don't think for a moment that I haven't considered the risk to the livelihood of salespersons like myself that some of the more controversial ideas expressed in this effort represent. As a third-generation Realtor®, I hold in high esteem the traditions of this industry and seek to preserve its integrity. However, whether we discuss it or not, the real estate industry is evolving.

## III

## My World

I work at the recession's core, Florida, where the subprime mortgage crisis inflicted some of the worst damage on property values. According to data from the fourth quarter of 2013, Florida was second only to Nevada in the number of mortgaged residential properties with negative equity (meaning that a borrower owed more on a home than it was worth). Orlando and Tampa were the two metro areas in the nation with the highest percentage of residences with negative equity: Orlando at 31.5 percent and Tampa at 30.4 percent. Fast forward to the second quarter of 2014, when the economy was "looking up," and the Lakeland/Winter Haven MSA (centered between Orlando and Tampa) was one of only two metros in the nation to experience negative growth. That probably explains why the area where I work has an average home sales price that is almost half that of the median-priced, US home. Home prices remain about 5 percent below their levels of eleven years ago. About 35 percent of all home sales involve distressed properties, REOs (real estate-owned by institutions, mostly foreclosures), or short sales (owners selling homes for less than the balance of their mortgages). Here, in this environment, real estate professionals have to do twice as much for

Realty Highway

half as much money (if they are lucky). Profitable? Who wants to sell real estate in this market? What notable national real estate company would want this?

Over the years, much of my residential real estate sales production has been from REO sales. Many REO properties are located in rural areas and are in deplorable condition. These properties must be cleaned up and often fixed up before they can be sold. We view or evaluate each property weekly, monthly, and quarterly; we secure and maintain utilities, assist with property upkeep, and much more. With each property, there is a monetary outlay by the real estate agent, usually thousands of dollars (reimbursed months later, although not always fully recoverable). There are many additional miscellaneous real estate office expenses, too, which can be much greater than the expenses of selling a non-REO property: such sales require more staff, supplies, advertising, and so on. All this and so much more are done in order to sell, in my area, properties with an average selling price under $100,000.

So where is the profit? When there is one, it's razor thin. Yet, I'm being wined and dined by some members of the top brass of a national firm, one that I'm already affiliated with and have been for years. While its financial officer works with members of my staff, other company executives are telling me that they really want to keep my little book of business and to capture more business like it. Really? Get out of here!

It is surreal to listen to them tell me how much they want my business to remain with them. In the midst of it, I am harkened back to conversations with similar executives years earlier, when a group purchasing our real estate company said to me "Why are you wasting your time with this type of business? It's not profitable. Focus on any other type of property." They were reacting upon a realization that a small portion of my personal residential business came from banks and other lending institutions, which generally indicates lower-end properties. That was fifteen years ago, when my partners and I sold our company, though I remained in my office to sell for that national brand.

Yet that conversation rang in clear contrast to the signal that the executives were sending to me today, as they were trying to figure out what I do and how to keep me, and my REO inventory, associated with them. What they wanted was more of what they didn't want fifteen years ago. Strange!

Why would a real estate company want REO business?

1) Calls and clicks result from the appearance of REO properties because the public perceives them as bargains. Are they good values? Could be. It's like the merchandise at any discount store: You can find good value, but unless you comparison shop each time you purchase, you are liable to overspend on some things. Firms marketing REO properties generally create a massive database of buyers, many of whom purchase multiple properties. These leads can last way beyond the purchase of a single REO property. Banks and institutions advertise nationally and internationally, which occurs in addition to the (often local) marketing of the listing real estate agent. Some financial institutions with many REO properties develop a following of buyers who then follow those REO properties across the country. Many real estate sales companies and agents tap into these prospects.

2) REO and short-sale business make up a greater share of the market than it did in years past. As a consequence, large institutions and governments are creating a greater footprint for themselves in

the marketplace. The percentage of owner-occupied homes is dropping as hedge fund and other investors continue to gobble up the properties hardest hit by the housing bubble. The banks continue to rely on the big institutions of Freddie Mac and Fannie Mae.

3) There is a sense that ongoing demographic and preference changes will continue to negatively impact the traditional real estate market. Consumers have many lifestyle choices, and the "Ten percent down, white picket fence house" that country singers Florida Georgia Line sing about has fewer takers. And some who do purchase, figure out later that it's not for them.

4) Finally, as upheavals such as a low- to no-growth rate and a shrinking workforce churn in the economy, as immigration issues metastasize, and as the economy continues to globalize, real estate will be affected and REO/short-sale business (or some variation of it) will maintain its large footprint on the traditional real estate market.

It's not my intention to detail this grand shift in market preference, and the psychology of it, nor to fully address the tepid economy we are experiencing. Rather, this book speaks to the related factors I confront almost daily and attempts to add context to such experiences.

# IV

# Perspectives

The subprime mortgage crisis continues to impact the US economy. For many, the pain has been so intense that it will not soon be forgotten. Preferences and buying patterns have changed as the effects of the crisis continue. Some have called it the Great Recession (with obvious reference to the Great Depression). Of course, stockbrokers are not currently jumping from windows. (Many Realtors might want to, but most have ground-level offices.) Stockbrokers, in fact, are enjoying record profits as a result of a bull market propped up by government policies. At the other end of the spectrum, the government provides a cushion from the total destitution many experienced during the Depression, which includes the extension of unemployment benefits, medical and housing benefits, supplemental food benefits, educational benefits, phones, and so on.

Of course, this is not a study of government's impact on society. The point is simply that government benefits exist at both ends of the financial spectrum. The government makes policies that support the growth of wealth and that contain an inherent expectation of continued growth. But with the existence of such benefits come consequences, such as an unhealthy dependence on government that could last for generations.

Laws protect us from the pain of extreme failure. Many decisions and actions within the financial market are made based on what the government is expected to do. Our massive government "wags the dog." Just watch the financial high rollers clamor to alter their portfolios after the chair of the Federal Reserve System's board of governors speaks. On the other end of the spectrum, don't you think that longer-lasting unemployment and other benefits figure into decisions made by the unemployed about what job to take?

I suppose it is a lot easier to request more government intervention than it is to take on the project of creating market solutions to our financial woes. I firmly believe that a more informed consumer, operating within a user-friendly and transparent marketplace, can lessen the need for government intervention and lower the chances of an economic meltdown. Note that I didn't say we could do away with government intervention, but simply *lessen* it. Instead of constantly looking to the government for help, today's industries should concentrate on developing and providing virtual tools for the public to assist them in making good decisions. They should try making the complex financials more understandable so that novices can participate in economic growth, and then examine the public's use of those tools. Unfortunately, most of the popular virtual applications developed help people manage their entertainment options or stock portfolios; few help manage the equity (or lack thereof) in their home.

Horace Mann (education reformer) said, Education then, beyond all other devices of human origin, is the great equalizer of the conditions of men, the balance-wheel of the social machinery." Information, properly presented, will equalize the playing field in the real estate market.

## J. Michael Nolen Jr.

Long before the subprime problem became apparent, there were statistical warning signs—not widely distributed—of the impending housing bust. All too many people (like some of my partners) received their information from those profiting from the feeding frenzy, rather than going straight to the source for real estate data (which, by the way, was then much more limited than it is today).

I think often of the day in 2006 when I sat across the conference table from my partners in a real estate development. I presented a very profitable offer from another developer. It was an opportunity for us to profit quickly, rather than via a long, drawn-out development process. At the time, prices were still going up, although the upward climb was not as steep. Of course, my general contractor partner would have the most to lose by us not building on the balance of the lots.

The building industry was all abuzz with "happy talk," and though there were some voices warning of trouble ahead, they were overpowered by the excitement. My presentation to my partners was insufficient to get them to see the train wreck ahead and to sell the land. Today, there is detailed supply-and-demand data going back well over a decade. At the time, though, market trends were harder to detect. I've often replayed the scenario in my mind, wondering whether the additional stats available to us today would have made a difference in my partners' decision to keep the land and not sell. The pain of regret I felt, watching a potentially healthy profit diminish to a 75 percent loss, has reshaped my financial perspective. We had leveraged our original purchase with a bank loan, so we took a real hit financially. Now, I try to avoid most debt.

As important as it is to obtain enough information, getting the context right and having it organized correctly so that the public can see how it directly impacts them is essential. We

Realty Highway

have that opportunity today: to improve on context. Think of how the hurricane spaghetti models, taking into consideration the many variables of the weather, are so helpful in explaining the probable direction hurricanes will travel. Economic models should be more like that. For example, they should indicate how potential interest rate fluctuations, tax code changes, US dollar value trends, and so forth might impact the broad housing market. Locally, probable property value trends could be forecasted as future land use or zoning changes, property tax rates changes, or the entrance of new industries into the area are proposed. From improved presentations and easier access to data, emerges a more engaged public.

People should have easy access to raw data, to diverse opinions, and to various charts signifying possible market movement. Unfortunately, government agencies and private industries sometimes benefit from a less-informed public. Additionally, it's hard to chart or predict the game-changing actions of government or large businesses.

In the panic of the Great Depression, my great-grandmother waited in a long line, only to have the South Side Bank close with only three people between her and the teller. Losing nearly $5,000 there, she then quickly ran to the Ensley Bank, only to find it closed. She lost another $45, which was all of her money. Like the 2008 real estate meltdown, it happened so quickly, yet there were signs of impending disaster. All around her town of Birmingham, Alabama, businesses, steel plants, and mines closed. As time went on, even the basic necessities became hard to get. At one point, my grandmother and great-grandmother went four days without food. For Christmas one year, their "big meal," actually their only meal, was a box of candy that a boyfriend had given my grandmother. Eventually, the Red Cross came to the rescue, but even then, there was a significant amount of red tape associated with the assistance.

*15*

## J. Michael Nolen Jr.

Today, those of us who are still experiencing the recession are not missing many meals, but the impact of the housing bubble (like that of the Great Depression) will not soon be forgotten. Living through years of negative or near-negative real estate values and minimal job creation can change a person, perhaps for life.

The largest home in the neighborhood I grew up in had a moat, an indoor pool, and a putting range. Business associates said that the owner made his money from purchasing real estate at the very low Great Depression prices. The government having auctioned off properties taken back for nonpayment of property taxes. These days, large hedge funds, most with multiple names, purchase real estate in large quantities at very low prices. Business failures are prevalent, as is the business practice of using part-time rather than full-time workers. The workforce participation numbers are low. The amount of government assistance distributed is high. All the while, the great divide between those of low and high net worth continues to grow ever wider.

Best I can tell, Wall Street's word for those of us who live in locations where it still feels like the Great Recession rather than the slowest recovery ever is "headwinds." The headwinds are slowing the economy from its movement toward prosperity.

All too often, the media portrayed those who fell victim to the real estate market collapse as people who lied on mortgage applications. But this mischaracterizes the vast majority of people who are hardworking and financially responsible and simply got caught up in the ripple effects of the prime mortgage disaster. At least that's how I have witnessed it. Which got me to wondering, how pervasive is this misperception across the country? Am I the only one who has experiences like these?

Members of my team once witnessed a suicide attempt by a man in a mobile home that was in foreclosure. He was not a

US citizen and could barely speak English. His spouse kept the foreclosure a secret from him until their personal effects had to be removed from the mobile home. Trying to communicate with the couple between tears and screams was a nightmare for my team. After the deputy left, the husband went into the bathroom, and then it really got crazy. After he had been in there for a while and did not respond to calls, someone broke into the bathroom in order to save him from certain death.

This type of scenario is very rare, fortunately. To the financial institution's credit, it did make some allowances for this couple. But many times, homeowners work with their mortgage company, make the three or four months of payments that the banker requests to avoid foreclosure, and still lose their home. Some were so sure that the bank was working *for* them that they didn't believe the notices I gave them until they received a three-day notice of eviction delivered by law enforcement. Many a neighbor has seen the contents of a home placed by the road, and even participated in the frenzy over all the "free" stuff, like vultures over roadkill.

Of course, the mortgage company isn't always the problem. Sometimes it's the companies that you see advertised on the Web that for a small fee, will work on your behalf with the lender to help you keep your house. Yep, they are your best buddies…not! Often, the "vulture" would take an upfront fee for their services and then do nothing. Fortunately, regulations have reduced these types of occurrences.

Still, many shady practices continue, and regulation and legislation have done little to alleviate them. It's not unusual for foreclosures to go before a judge, who encourages both parties (the lender and property owner) to work out a loan modification in lieu of foreclosure. The bank then makes it so difficult for the property owner to speak to anyone but a machine that nothing ever happens. The foreclosure sale date comes and goes. The homeowner is then notified of the eviction. In these cases, the homeowner moves away, sad and discouraged. Sometimes, the bank offers a small amount of cash for moving expenses and to discourage further litigation.

Now, to be fair, I often only get one side of the story, and it's not my place to investigate the property owner's point of view. But I have witnessed employees of mortgage companies with huge workloads and lenders that have been victims of vandalism, probably originated by disgruntled homeowners. Bankers often find that their recently foreclosed homes have been stripped of electrical wiring, kitchen cabinets, counters, even toilets, with holes in every wall and ceiling, and even entire walls removed by the homeowners. When the mortgage company first enters a house that has been foreclosed upon, there is no telling what it will find. Sometimes the homes have significant water damage. A number of times, I've walked into houses that, from floor to ceiling, display black "discoloration" caused by the intrusion of water into the house. Some are like going into a cave. Just awful. And people wonder why banks can be so protective of their real estate interests.

But it's the stories of the homeowners that pull at the heart. I hear stories like the one about "Mary," a mobile-home owner, middle-aged, with one older child. When I met her, it was easy to see that she took pride in her abode. She had renovated the kitchen and made various other improvements to her modest home.

Mary worked as a waitress in a local, family-owned business, living "hand to mouth." Each year, the restaurant would close for a month while the family visited Europe. Unfortunately, during that time the staff did not get a full month's pay. Of course, life still happens, and Mary had issues with her home, including her air conditioner breaking. After years of timely monthly payments, she missed a month. Then, the bank became difficult to deal with. Finally, a judge stepped in and ordered the two parties to work together on a loan modification. All parties to the transaction reached an agreement. But that was virtually the last time that the homeowner spoke directly to a person at the bank. Apparently, the bank had no one that could spend quality time with her to assist in the loan modification process. That is, until the foreclosure sale date when, miraculously, her modification was approved. By then, it was too late.

I have sat across tables from many fine folks who found themselves in financial trouble. I remember one delightful family, a husband and wife with stairstep children. The oldest two had been employed in the family business. The father bragged about their efforts in the family business, obviously proud of his children, but embarrassed by the situation he now found himself in. The young ones seemed not to understand what was happening. The parents treated the meeting like a big adventure to try to save them from the pain. A few years before, their house, a contemporary, 3,000-square-foot home with a pool and a large detached office/warehouse serving as headquarters for their small business, had been valued at half a million dollars.

Today, this compound of sorts wasn't worth much more than $200,000, I thought, as he showed me around, noting with pride the custom touches he had made, and then acting embarrassed at the plumbing problems that were never fixed, as evidenced by the holes and exposed pipes in the walls. In private, he whispered his only request of me: that I not place a notice over the door that he would have to explain to his youngest kids, who were around seven years old.

His business was now a shadow of its former prominence, he related. He felt compelled to tell me about his business locations, which one by one had shut down as his clientele fell into hard times. Then he emptied the office/warehouse next to his home as the business continued to slide. I asked him where he would go. "It's hard. Rent is expensive for a home to meet our minimal needs." He went on to tell me about a small retail outlet his family would still maintain while they strove to rebuild the business.

Besides the home, and sometimes even more than the home, losing the family business can hurt the most, especially when your hope is to pass it on to future generations. Multigenerational dreams are lost. It's one thing to lose a business because of missed calculations or a lack of effort, but it's quite another to lose it because of the actions of others, caused the market to collapse, with no improvement in sight.

Many people lost their life's savings in the dot-com bust; it was awful. But mostly they lost their savings. Those caught up in the subprime bust often lost their homes. Losing a home is heartbreaking. It's not easy to overcome. And for those who lost businesses, well, it's beyond disheartening.

Everyone in our area either had financial setbacks or knew of someone who did. Most of them have yet to recover from it. The pervasive nature of the decline in real estate values significantly affects real estate sales and ripples across other sectors of the economy and into the lives of many. Some will suffer long-lasting physical and psychological effects. This all creates turmoil and in turn exposes weaknesses in the processes of selling, purchasing, financing, and owning real estate.

From these horrid conditions come watered-down dreams, with life preferences newly constructed around risk-avoidance. Risk-avoidance taken to the extreme, in turn, sets one up to be devoured by the jaws of inflation. Placing one's money under the mattress might keep it from getting lost, but inflation will eat away at its value. Then, through it all, discouragement sets in, creating an endless cycle wherein the passion to try again can be lost. Still, if the business of real estate were to undergo a transformation, and be user-friendly enough, some people burned last time around will lift their heads up from last decade's recession to have another real estate experience.

With appropriate education and properly applied technology, the healing process can take place. Executed correctly, a movement massively altering the processes involved with the exchange of real estate can occur. The time is right, and there has been enough pain that the public will welcome significant change. I believe they will soak up the information. "Build it and they will come," to quote *Field of Dreams*. If such a transformation is marketed correctly, even real estate professionals will embrace it.

# V

# Preferences

The Preamble to the National Association of Realtors Code of Ethics begins, "Under all is the land. Upon its wise utilization and widely allocated ownership depend the survival and growth of free institutions and of our civilization...the interest of the nation and its citizens require the highest and best use of the land and the widest distribution of land ownership. They require the creation of adequate housing, the building of functioning cities, the development of productive industries and farms, and the preservation of a healthful environment."

I have witnessed among many people (expressed verbally and behaviorally) a sentiment implying that the concepts expressed in the Preamble are outdated and perhaps better suited for an agrarian society or, at the very least, an America before the housing bust. That's anecdotal, perhaps, but it's an attitude voiced more today than in years past. Of course, this might change as rents continue increasing, but for now, owning real estate (for all too many people in our area) is seen as a barrier to personal freedom. Some say, it's detrimental to their financial solvency. In a day and age of mobility, I can see why some would feel chained to their homes, which for many are still not worth as much as their mortgage. Sadly, for too many, the American dream of a home on a piece of ground has become a nightmare.

For a variety of reasons, many see real estate as being tarnished; others would say it's on life support. Kevin O'Leary, investor and television personality, told CNCB's Michelle Fox that rising interest rates will "rip through the infrastructure of utilities, and REITS and real estate…Don't buy any real estate. Don't do it." And some have heeded his advice, as reported by the *Daily Real Estate News*. Dean Baker, codirector of the Center for Economic and Policy Research in Washington, DC, says, "Home ownership for all age groups has fallen to 64.8 percent, the lowest level since 1995."

Consider the Millennials, defined by the US Chamber of Commerce Foundation as those born between 1980 and 1999. The decline in homeownership of this age bracket has been widely reported, with the greatest drop being among those aged twenty-five to twenty-nine. With interest rates and home prices still very low, these young people, traditionally, would be buying homes, especially given the knowledge that eventually the Feds will tighten the money supply.

The influence that the Feds usurp on interest rates is one of their most powerful tools for regulating the economy. After virtually every Fed meeting, business media like CNBC discuss at length the probability of interest rates going up. The rates *will* increase; it's just a matter of when. Very soon after I started selling real estate, the prevailing interest rates charged by banks on home mortgages rose to about 18 percent. Talk about a bad real estate market! As you can imagine, sales dropped to extreme lows. But interest rates do not have to undergo drastic change to have an effect on the economy. Even small changes in interest rates can significantly impact the affordability of real estate.

J. Michael Nolen Jr.

A couple of reasons that Millennials are not purchasing homes in great numbers are the volume of debt many struggle with and the time it takes to grow credit scores. Although balances on some types of debt have dropped overall, student loans continue to be an issue. The Federal Reserve Bank reported that the totals in student loans for those younger than thirty have grown from 220 billion in 2007 to 322 billion in 2012. During that period, those under thirty who were more than ninety days delinquent on payments rose from 4.9 percent to nearly 9 percent. Those older than thirty have an even higher delinquency rate.

Many young people have increased their debt in efforts to further their education and realize increased prospects of a high-paying job. At the same time, wages in the United States are essentially stagnant; the part-time labor force is growing, the employment participation rate is low, and business failures are increasing. So, in many fields of endeavor, it's hard to make that education investment work.

While student debt was encouraged, the path to home financing was simultaneously tightened. Credit requirements have increased, and the financing costs of low-down-payment mortgages have increased.

In a survey by Ipsos Public Affairs for Wells Fargo & Company, eighteen- to thirty-four-year-olds ranked having a down payment as the biggest impediment to purchasing a home. Forty-four percent knew nothing or very little about closing costs. And of course, unless they're in the mortgage-lending business, they don't understand that the cost of originating a loan continues to go up and, in some form or another, is passed on from the lender to the consumer.

It's amazing how little the public knows about purchasing real estate, especially given the abundance of information that is available. Of course, many young adults have no interest in

## Realty Highway

purchasing a home, and think that it's something to do when you're ready to settle down and maybe have children. Eighteen- to thirty-four-year-olds, meanwhile, are apparently less inclined than previous generations to marry and have children, as indicated by the growing number of singles in this category.

Next is the "cool" factor. Has real estate lost its coolness for many? As silly as that sounds, it makes a difference, especially for the young. Part of the appeal of Apple products, after all, is their coolness.

The media spends untold hours contemplating the perceived value of innovative technology, much of which has not even reached the market. The stock market soars as big corporate money chases technological breakthroughs. The public lines up outside of stores for hours waiting for the newest innovations in phones and wearables. TV screens are growing ever bigger. Consumers chase fashionable headphones and laptops with the Apple logos prominently displayed on the back. It's fast paced and cool.

It's easy to see why people are apt to believe that the survival and growth of free institutions and of our civilization rely upon the wide availability of and the wisest use of information and technology, and not on land. Innovative technology and vast amounts of information are so readily available to us, impacting our personal lives so profoundly, that they have affected the very context we use to view our lives.

Don't you think that there are those who have more allegiance to their Twitter followings or Facebook friends (entities with no borders) than to their own country (a land with borders)? Innovative technology offers, for many, a sense of newfound freedom. Its freedom of everything—from where to work and live, to a choice of escape (just pick your game or other visual), or to go wherever or do whatever, virtually. No longer (for many) is it necessary to work from nine to five in a traditional brick-and-mortar office; neither do you have to actually be there in person to work or to maintain relationships with family and friends. Individuals can seemingly choose their environment on a whim. Portable computing and wearable devices fit this paradigm perfectly. So it stands to reason that time and money, once spent to purchase and maintain a home or office, is rather feeding this paradigm of portability. Money is being diverted to the entertainment and technology sectors of the economy. Many people upgrade their phone or computer with nearly every new product; it's hard to do that with a house.

Of course, this could all be a fad. But for now, the real estate world that the Preamble alluded to seems dull and passé.

Now, to be fair, the real estate sector does have its own very popular TV channel, HGTV (not counting programs like *Flip That House*, which aired prior to the housing bust). And there are ever-improving online services like Zillow, CoreLogic, Realtor.com, and so on. And obviously, real estate is always a part of the economy. For example, the iPhone you are using was assembled in buildings of brick and mortar, and the café where you use your Wi-Fi may be the highest and best current use of real estate. Even if you are renting a condo or living in your parents' basement, it's still real estate. Obviously, people still want to buy homes. However, the typical three-bedroom, two-bath home on a quarter-acre lot in an older neighborhood without amenities is not as popular as it once was (particularly if it's old). Unless buyers have or plan to have more than one child, they often prefer to live in resort-type communities or areas with quality amenities.

# VI

# Ignorance

So, that said, perhaps the traditional use of land is not in vogue and, OK, it's not as profitable as in days' past. Neither is using computers manufactured a decade ago.

The question is, what needs are currently *not* being met in the real estate market? Well, of course, profit would be nice, and maybe some equity accumulation. Certainly, those are the endgame, but an injection of some of what makes Silicon Valley products popular would be nice, too. An infusion of innovation, perhaps? If those who deliver the innovation (eighteen- to thirty-four-year-olds) don't even understand the basic closing costs associated with buying real estate, much less the process of purchasing it, the place to start is with good information or content. This is generally understood in the real estate industry. For example, consider Rupert Murdoch's News Corp's acquisition of Move, Inc., a mix of Rupert's news content with Move's real estate websites such as Realtor.com, ListHub, and Top Producer.com (a real estate customer-relations management system, or CRM). Considerably less attention is paid to how ignorance negatively impacts the real estate industry, and why something isn't being done about it. Because both buyers and sellers have a limited understanding of the real estate market and the transaction process, they can become frustrated with the real estate professional, the industry, and the entire process of buying, selling, or renting a property, especially when the transaction does not occur the way they envision it. The professional likes that feeling, the mystique, of making a little miracle (a purchase, sale, or rental) happen, with the customer not really knowing how it all occurred. real estate professionals, in fact, fear customers knowing too much about their jobs. The theory is, if customers know too much, they will decide to do without such professional services.

I think the situation is just the opposite: The more customers know about the services rendered, and the more engaged they are in the process, the more they will want a professional's involvement, and the easier the transaction will become.

The same fear abounded when the Multiple Listing Service (MLS) search website and Craigslist first became available, and when discount brokers became so prevalent. Many professionals thought these developments would be detrimental to business. Instead, they have made our professions easier. Often today, when customers find their way to a professional, much of the search work has already been done, and they have a greater appreciation for the professional's services. It will work the same way for all the other parts of a real estate transaction. Really, as busy as people are, do you think they also have time to do a financial or real estate professional's job?

Information is a good thing. Now, I can hear you saying, "Slow down...now hold on, we do explain the process to our customers."

But the information we give our customers has to be much more than simply a verbal laundry list of items needed or things to do, or a cursory review of the process. Or, need I say, more than a new government form (government regulations and forms change all the time—with nary an improvement).

The conveyance has to be visual, too, with charts and projections, simplified instructions, a brief history of why the real estate transaction is the way it is and how the closing process flows, including an overview of the entire process. It needs to be condensed, yet expansive (you know, a picture tells a thousand words) and easy to understand.

The more customers know, the easier the transactions and the higher the success rates. True, maybe they won't buy the more expensive home, or maybe they will wait to purchase until they've accumulated a larger down payment. But that's a good thing. A more educated customer assists the professional, helping him or her make better decisions. With more informed decisions comes a more stable economy and reduced likelihood of another real estate crash.

The content must be fully accessible (cheap or free and user-friendly), timely, pertinent to the real estate market, and organized, all presented with full transparency and perhaps a flair of "coolness."

Of course, cheap or free content, much to the chagrin of the publishing industry, is virtually everywhere. Everyone knows that content is king in driving traffic to websites, and so it's omnipresent.

As for timely content: Can you get much quicker than a Twitter feed?

## VII

## Information

Real estate-related content that is organized and germane has only recently gained in popularity, and there is still a lot of room for improvement. A good start is HomeZada.com®, purported to "manage your digital home...A personal finance solution that is a digital hub of all the important information about your largest financial asset—your home." Among other things, the site keeps track of improvements made and maintenance both scheduled and completed on the home. One can even place property for sale on the site and transfer the records kept on the house to the new owners.

 I say "good start" because there is so much more real estate-related information available but not easily within the grasp of the public. The public, in fact, has little awareness of the amount and type of information available to real estate professionals: market-watch reports showing properties recently placed on the market, properties with recent contracts accepted by the seller, properties fallen off the market, and so forth. Professionals are also privy to data broken down by community, zip code, and neighborhood. In fact, available stats can be further categorized—by number of bedrooms and baths, year of construction, square footage, and much more, allowing for customized stats and specific property value estimates. Individual property characteristics, such as lake or canal frontage, close proximity to airports or historic districts, and so forth, can also be considered when automating real estate value estimates and tracking values.

Additionally, mortgage rates can be tracked, signaling when to lock in rates. real estate professionals also have dashboards, tracking timed events or providing task reminders, to make sure that every part of a sales transaction is completed on time and in order. Of course, there are easy fill-in contracts galore, designed for every imaginable type of real estate transaction and disclosure and disclaimer forms of every kind. All the forms and property stats are updated either daily or as required.

Links…wow, are there links! A very small sampling of online resources includes school reports, property zoning maps and definitions, flood maps, lists of fifty-five-and-older communities, a real estate dictionary, foreclosure and preforeclosure maps, property tax information, and special financing information, including up-to-the-minute rate changes, and more.

You may think, "This is too much to handle without a professional." Perhaps. Not to be disparaging to my profession though, it's hardly rocket science.

However, my real point is that this information should be readily available to the public, appropriately organized, with real estate professionals then acting as advisors. The public should be encouraged to take more interest in the real estate market, and see firsthand the impact of various factors that influence it.

To accomplish this, it is proposed that a comprehensive real estate dashboard be developed for the general public. Realty Highway, as we call it, would be organized into six parts:

- Organizing the news and voices of the real estate and related sectors
- Stats
- How-to: transaction-centered content
- Directory
- Searches
- Purchasing

While Google and other search engines turn up such information, alas it is scattered at best.

With Realty Highway, there would be organization to the news and voices of real estate and its related fields.

It's interesting to work with young buyers and sellers. Their understanding of the real estate market often comes from HGTV, Zillow, Realtor.com®, Google, property tax records, and the advice of friends. These are all important resources, and they collectively represent so much more information than previous generations had access to. Still, even with all that information, they lack a basic understanding of real estate principles and processes.

Too many voices are out there all speaking at once. Although we may not be able to organize properly the entire Internet, we *can* begin the process of organizing real estate and related content on the Internet. That collection of voices should be a virtual library of trade magazines, news, commentary, and blogs; absolutely everything real estate, or that touches upon real estate, should be consolidated. Additionally, the effort should include news and views that can be customized to the taste of the reader, cutting through the clutter of the many voices. As such, it should provide intuitive content delivery, guiding the public along in fields or services of interest.

I recommend The News Funnel®, which provides an excellent start toward compiling a virtual library to serve as one component of the public's personal real estate dashboard, or Realty Highway. The News Funnel does a good job of cutting through the barrage of headline-grabbing news articles, websites, and blogs clamoring for your attention and brings its customers customized content. Customers get to choose which local markets they wish to follow, as well as subject areas they're interested in. In our case, interests could include such topics as finance, market forecast, REIT, architecture, and so on.

As described on its website, The News Funnel works by gathering "trade news and information from trusted industry sources and then [letting] users craft that information into a custom feed." CoreLogic, meanwhile, is another vendor that is developing and offering apropos content, including MLS stats across multiple and related sectors.

This type of product, properly organized, broadly based, all-inclusive, with added intuitiveness, would constitute a virtual library, with updates delivered daily, as well as a stationary reference as part of its patrons' virtual dashboard.

Like any movement, this one needs a leader. This is particularly true if one of the goals is to unite the real estate market with all that touches it into one central dashboard serving as a virtual hub, a primary source linking the real estate industry with its many ancillary businesses, services, and regulating agencies. Here are some of the benefits such a dashboard would provide:

- Proper organization of information and clear explanations of services, including the relationships between the various services, to better serve both professionals and the public
- Cohesion, increased efficiency, and transparency among those industries that touch or influence the real estate economy
- Promotion of public understanding of the real estate economy and an increase in the number of options available to its patrons

Dashboard content should be objective, representing many viewpoints (all are welcome), yet cradled in the writings of respected professionals in each of the major fields represented. It should be all about content, but also provide context, presenting a narrative that includes all related industries. It should *not* be about selling website design, CRMs, or anything else, nor should it be simply a place to access real estate Multiple Listing Services.

All around us is an abundance of content in the various media; what is needed is organization. Content should be geared both to the general public and to professionals and organized into five broad classifications, within which would be a series of faceted classifications. Wikipedia® describes faceted classification as a system that allows "the assignment of an object to multiple taxonomy (sets of attributes), enabling the classification to be ordered in multiple ways, rather than in a single, predetermined, and taxonomic order."

Here are the basic classifications:

- Land and that which improves and enhances the land for personal usage (residential buildings, fences, furniture, gardens, and so on)

## Realty Highway

- That which maintains, protects, and ensures the improvements
- That which defines and influences it (laws, government regulations, terminology, trends, locations, and so on)
- That which facilitates the purchase, lease, exchange, and sale of it (financing, multiple listing services—divided between commercial/securities and residential categories, title services, and so on)
- All things pertaining to what is derived from it (income, commercial use, and so on)

Readers can thus link directly to those areas of the website that are of the greatest interest to them, customizing the news and views they receive daily, including whatever pertains primarily to their locales. Because real estate values are defined more by local happenings than national events, the real estate hub would bring the two together: national and local news.

There are many ways to generate income from within such an organized system and still keep it free or nearly free for patrons.

# VIII

## Stats

All relevant stats need to be collected within the dashboard and automatically updated. This would include government-maintained stats as well as those of private services such as the Multiple Listing Services. Both macro and micro stats should be included (reaching from nationwide in scope down to individual neighborhoods). The data needs to be raw, with linked interpretations of the data remaining in the blog section.

Charts like those that predict hurricanes could then track the economy. Like the maps following each precinct in an election, stats related to real estate supply and price per square foot per MSA and county, among other data, could be placed at readers' fingertips.

This information is readily available now, but unless it is paid for, it has to be pieced together. Generally, unless you go straight to the source, such information comes with commentary; that commentary often conveniently omits information that might contradict the writer's opinion. Of course, commentary is fine in its place, as long as users have full access to the complete raw data.

# Realty Highway

Technology is available to bring the real estate sector, which is driven primarily by small local markets, to a central national exchange, where properties can be both considered within the framework of the local community and easily viewed from a macro perspective. Aside from real estate, many ancillary products and services also can be cost-analyzed and compared locally and nationally.

To gain context, users must be able to toggle easily between the details surrounding recent history as well as perspectives going back decades. Also, users should easily be able to navigate between micro and macro data.

Consider the presidential election process, and pollsters reaching down and analyzing details within even the smallest precincts. They then relate the data back to the national races and piece it all together. Like that coverage, this service needs to be free. Advertisements and internal links from the directory would pay for it.

# IX

## Transaction-Centered

Information can be organized around real estate-closing activities, such as one of the services I use, which creates various tasks to be checked upon completion as the transaction progresses.

In the real estate business, it's the closing transaction that counts. You can do a fine job of showing property, negotiating the contract, and preparing and organizing all the ancillary documents and services, but if the contract does not close, it's all for nothing.

Do not confuse this task-toward-closing function with the organization of news and views I mentioned earlier. This is a detailed how-to instruction, illustrated and with a tutorial explaining to the public the exact steps of the transaction.

The public is often confused by the many tasks that the various professionals complete to bring a closing to fruition. In fact, however, the tasks are straightforward and relatively simple. But just Google "steps to completing a real estate transaction" (or anything like it) for a more confused picture. You'll find many companies and industry leaders who will explain to you the steps to the successful closing of a real estate transaction…none are alike and none are comprehensive. Each statement about closing is made from the perspective of the one doing the telling. Of course, there are variations from state to state, variations related to cash transactions and types of financing, and so on. And, too, procedures change from time to time. So the closing experience described accurately is hardly a few paragraphs in Wikipedia; rather, it is a reference manual, with a tutorial displayed as a simple transaction model, that can expand with the click of a mouse to include the many and sundry issues that can arise during the closing process. Of course, no model would be complete without the inclusion of the various regulatory agencies that encumber the real estate industry. There's a lot to take in but, still, it's not rocket science.

The proposed website would be tasked with enabling those who would like to close real estate transactions for themselves with the information needed to do so, as well as with providing knowledge needed to simply check on the actions of professionals.

Information relating to postclosing activities could be included, such as rekeying the house, adding security systems, moving, buying furniture, decorating, landscaping, and so forth. All such activities could be linked to companies or professionals in the directory.

# X
# Directories

Directories consist of alphabetical listings of businesses that perform the various services associated with a real estate transaction.

The real estate industry has long been a proponent of the one-stop shop closing experience, with title insurance, mortgage finance, and real estate sales companies seamlessly working together. Consumers like the convenience and ease of it. In practice, however, the results have been far from spectacular. Often, each arm of the transaction varies in quality; or there can be a sense of collusion on the part of consumers (even when in reality it is nonexistent). Still, company reputations can be damaged by the mistakes of others and the things that are outside of their direct control.

Every applicable (local, regional, and national) company should be included without charge in the directory. Also, a brief description of what each company does, as well as a quick review ranking, should be available at the hover of a mouse. The inclusion of additional information could be offered to companies for a fee, similar to the method employed by the Yellow Pages.

# XI

## Searches

The path to closing a real estate deal begins with the search. Typically, that means a search for properties previously placed on the market for sale.

Homeowners allow real estate brokers to represent them in selling or renting their property. Licensed real estate agents photograph the real estate and gather information about it, and then place the property on the market for sale or rent. Properly vetted real estate brokers, in attempting to sell the property, place its information in a Multiple Listing Service (MLS), allowing other real estate agents and their customers to search for and view the homeowner's property information. When the property is sold or rented, the real estate broker is paid for his or her service.

In one organization's words, the MLS is formed to "promote, establish, foster, develop, and preserve the highest standards of the real estate profession…(it's) a means by which authorized Participants make blanket unilateral offers of compensation to other Participants…by which cooperation among participants is enhanced; by which information is accumulated and disseminated to enable authorized Participants to prepare appraisals, analyses, and other valuations of real property for bona fide clients and customers; by which Participants engaging in real estate appraisal contribute to common databases; and is a facility for the orderly correlation and dissemination of listing information so participants may better serve their clients and the public." The MLS is the epicenter for search information.

However, that MLS (or the brokers who hired the vendor who created the MLS product) and its respective homeowner (who signs a consent) allow other vendors (such as Zillow. com, Homes.com, and many Realtors® with private websites) to distribute much of this information on the Internet. These vendors distribute the details of properties for sale and sell advertising to other vendors, including real estate brokers. The real estate brokers purchase space on webpages in an effort and in a manner that gives the public an impression that they are the parties listing the property for sale. real estate brokers who advertise like this on the Internet would virtually never receive permission to do the same in print media. Often oblivious to the nuances, the prospective buyer calls the real estate broker running the advertisement to find additional information on the listed property, rather than the real estate agent who is working directly with the homeowner.

Once vendors like Zillow.com, Trulia.com, and Facebook get involved, homeowners and their real estate brokers (to a degree) both lose control of their housing information. Advertising real estate agents do not have the same knowledge of the listed property as do agents who work directly with the homeowner. Now, to be fair, some Realtor® associations enforce rules drafted to better distinguish listing agents from the advertisers. Still, the information-control issue remains. And information taken from some real estate search vendors can be inaccurate or dated. Of course, in order for a homeowner to have access to the more detailed searches of MLS, a real estate professional must provide the access.

No doubt, Realtors® and the MLS vendors who serve them are the leaders of the real estate industry. The MLS contains a wealth of information concerning the real estate market; if only such details were better distributed. Much of the distribution of really detailed MLS searches depend upon the competency and marketing savy of the individual real estate professional. Generally, the traditional system, with real estate professionals representing homeowners (or providing some form of representation), has served the public admirably for generations. This is so in large part because Realtors® organizations police ethical issues among their own. It's done so thoroughly, in fact, that there is little need for additional government oversight. They even go so far as to monitor and educate government "knuckleheads" about how their actions, or inactions, impact real estate values and private property rights.

This system for handling real estate transactions (including the MLS search feature and data collection) works. So the question becomes: Why fix something that's not broken? Which is followed by the next question: Does this mean that there's no room for a competing system? Perhaps, but maybe not.

What about the idea of locking up the sensitive information, as happens with the names of law enforcement officers, showing instruction and so forth, and then trusting homeowners with their own housing information? Huh? Look, it's just a thought. The advantage of entrusting homeowners with their own real estate dealings is that they would be more engaged in the process.

Their information could be slipped right into Realty Highway's MLS, or directly into a Facebook® MLS controlled by the property owner. Homeowners could upload photos and information about their properties and real estate agents could be optional. Yes, there are already options that allow homeowners to participate in an MLS as a for sale by owner. These systems like Zillow.com® are primitive, lacking many features available to real estate professionals. With Realty Highway and at the individual homeowner's discretion, a real estate professional could do it all or none of it; or the agent could be an advisor, or one who certifies the information that the homeowner provides. A real estate agent's service could remain important to the real estate transaction in many ways, but the homeowner would be in charge of the MLS process without necessarily having it go through a gatekeeper, by proxy or Realtor®. All homebuyers with this function on their computers would have their property searches updated each day according to their very detailed search criteria, and they would have access to the data compiled from both their and other property owners' transactions. There is so much to do in a typical real estate transaction that it is unlikely that real estate brokers would be affected too much from such described changes in MLS. They may, however, need a more flexible fee schedule.

But the concept I am discussing here is not the flat fee for real estate services that is already prevalent. Many companies offer a flat-fee service. Zillow claims these flat-fee services "are...offered through For Sale by Owner real estate websites that will get you the same exposure as agent-represented homes for a fraction of the cost. Average prices range from $299-$499 (based on local conditions). For this amount, you get listed on your local MLS, Realtor.com® (only homes in the MLS can be published on Realtor.com®), AOL, MSN, Yahoo and many more real estate websites that feature MLS listings." Zillow continues, "No commissions are paid to the listing (seller's) agent—your flat fee replaces the...commission you would normally pay in a contractual agreement." This is not what I am offering for your consideration.

Of course, with social media sites permeating society, it's all the more feasible for the MLS to bypass the Realtor® associations and many other real estate service vendors. There would be little need for them, because the Realty Highway application and dashboard would be desirable enough that each interested party's computer would have them. In addition to offering maximum real estate content, Realty Highway would stay up to date with the most advanced search features, most notably "lifestyle" searches. These searches might include property searches based around personal interests (fishing, flying, skiing, tourist attractions, and so forth) or built around certain employment or cultural interests.

Onboard Informatics is a great example of an improved, tech-savvy search. This next-generation listing platform has "filter and sort results...using twenty-five different fields including distance from a desired starting point, nearest transit, school rating, neighborhood name...it allows visitors to put a piece of property in the context of the surrounding area."

Online search quality is improving, opening up new options, including better quantifying locational aspects and adding context to other local facts and figures. Examples include searches that don't just locate lakes, but find lakes allowing seaplane landings, or airboats, or that have boat ramps, or even lakes of a certain depth. In particular, rural areas would benefit from better lifestyle searches. Rural areas are often overlooked in the searches of those living in urban areas. Lifestyle searches may reveal areas in which a real estate agent, working with a buyer or renter, may not even be aware exist.

An oversimplified but valid example nonetheless follows: A home in the popular area of Winter Park, just northeast of Orlando, Florida, is about thirty-seven minutes away from the Orlando International Airport. However, what could be easily overlooked is that west of Orlando, but less known even to Orlando locals, is Davenport, where travel time to OIA is about thirty-nine minutes. The average selling price of homes in Winter Park is about $200 per square foot. In Davenport, the average home sells for around $100 per square foot. Gaining this type of comparative data is not as easy as you might expect. It takes effort, too much effort given today's technology. Now, granted, Davenport may not be Winter Park when it comes to culture or the old-style estates. Still, for many, there are other lifestyle perks that are just as important, such as Davenport's seventeen-minute drive to Disney World®. (Winter Park is about thirty-five minutes away.) Unless Davenport is on the radar, though, buyers may not even consider it.

To supplement appraisals, banks and financial institutions use services such as Zillow to estimate property values. In my experience, valuations derived in this manner (without the assistance of a real estate appraiser) are often off-the-charts bad, though Zillow's website will tell you differently. I reviewed one such value for a waterfront house. The bank's automated evaluation (Zillow) was $350,000. My estimate of market value was $750,000. Just a *little* difference. Zillow and other vendors that assist with valuations do well with "cookie-cutter" homes, but everything else, not so much. Although such vendors have improved over the years, I'm still shocked that they aren't better.

In order to pinpoint an initial specific value for one's home and to detail the various factors that influence the property's evaluation, a professional's advice should be sought. Then the automation process is put into place that keeps track of the value. Periodically, the professional would check the automated value and adjust, or tweak, the value (and perhaps the criteria), and then reset the automation.

Suffice it to say, there is a need for better quality search features and a more accurate use of data.

However, these superior searches have their critics. Some express concerns that the additional data will "help Americans further self-sort into like-minded communities, or, worse increase segregation" (Karen Wise, reporting on a four-part series by Teke Wiggin of Inman News). Wiggin writes, "The proliferation of hyperlocal data will exacerbate the historical trend of wealthy people settling in affluent neighborhoods, pushing middle class into less high-end areas, and forcing people in already distressed neighborhoods to cope with a diminishing tax base. Beyond school ratings and crime data, more and more sites and apps are showing information like median income, political contributions, and the percentage of families with children, and racial composition at a hyperlocal level. Some of this data may undermine the spirit of fair housing laws, which have made many agents leery of disclosing information on protected classes like racial groups for fear of illegally steering them. It'll also make it easier for people to sort themselves into communities based on their values and beliefs, feeding the growth of like-minded neighborhoods."

OK, so what is the alternative? Is it to proclaim that Realtors® become more of a gatekeeper than they already are? How are they supposed to know what information they can reveal and what they are to hide? Really, that type of information has been used by commercial brokerages for decades (although receiving it wasn't as easy as hovering over it with a mouse pointer). Will there ever be a time when the American people can be trusted to make decisions that are not based on racial or similar discrimination? If so, what is the threshold for it? For, if a very high standard is set, I guess the only remedy is increased dependence on gatekeepers.

# XII

# Purchases

Auction companies are getting better and better at giving real estate buyers the information they need to buy property online without necessarily viewing it. With an abundance of real estate and community information, as well as the use of algorithms, complex automated searches, and perhaps "certified inspectors" or "certified verifications," buyers can purchase with confidence. Contracts often provide buyers protection, with due diligence periods and financing contingencies.

Real estate crowdfunding is growing in popularity. Realty Mogul created a "marketplace for accredited investors to pool money online and buy shares of prevetted investment properties." Using their platform, investors "with as little as $5,000" can participate with "like-minded investors to make investments that are otherwise difficult to access."

Auctions and crowdfunding can add a measure of liquidity to real estate. Liquidity is one of the advantages that the stock market has over the real estate market.

# XIII

## Possibilities

As the Realty Highway and social media merge the possibilities are limitless. You could invite others into your virtual home to share conversation, a game, a movie, decorating ideas, to see the various Facebook® pages of each household member, and so on. Your personal, virtual resource for real estate information could allow an audience access to additional information about your property or to see what real estate-related services professionals you recommend. For example, if you didn't know which professional on the directory to use, with a click you could go to the site of someone you respect and see who he or she recommends from their directory. Designed properly, this resource could speed up distribution of the Realty Highway, particularly if homeowners had to limit the number of professionals in each field that they could recommend. The goal of a young professional could be to be recommended by as many well-established, respected professionals as possible. And since the well-established professional is limited to recommending three insurance salesmen (for example), the race is on.

Included on your real estate dashboard would be applications for real estate equity accounts with values that are continually updated, along with mortgage amortization and depreciation reductions, all more accurate than the various vendors offer today, and perfect for real estate 401K accounts.

You could operate your smart home from your real estate dashboard and keep track of likely expenses over the years (for example, closely estimating the life expectancy of appliances, air conditioning, and so on, and the costs to replace them), all totaled up to estimate the true cost of a household. You could prepare and keep more accurate budgets. This feature alone could reduce the number of foreclosures. Who knows what else such a virtual real estate platform might facilitate? Hey...I think this could even be cool.

# XIV

# Alternatives

It's interesting to see MLS vendors continue to increase the number of features they offer to Realtors® and their customers. The majority of Realtors® work for small companies, and they appreciate the many added features. On the other hand, larger real estate offices have offered their associates the same or similar features for a long time (though at a high cost). Now, the small real estate offices are receiving these features essentially for free because they are included within the fees normally paid for MLS benefits. So to sum up, as larger companies pay their MLS fees, they assist their competition.

The traditional real estate companies (many with large management hierarchies) have to compete with countless new companies (often small ones), with lower overhead, and that offer employees 401(k)s and profit-sharing options, while charging only desk costs. With lots of overhead, the large real estate companies are constantly looking for other competitive advantages. Many set their sights on the high-end market, which is one reason I have been surprised at their interest in REO properties. Frequently, newly licensed real estate agents place their licenses with large traditional firms first. After they are trained, they are generally persuaded to move to discount brokerages, where they receive at or near 100 percent commissions.

Another problem is low and stagnant real estate prices, which have taken a bite out of real estate brokers' commissions.

Commercial brokers, too, operate under challenging circumstances, with e-commerce having altered the commercial landscape. It's interesting: In an effort to distinguish themselves from real estate agents specializing in residential properties, commercial brokers offer their own MLS of sorts, which cost more than, yet are inferior to, residential MLS. Go figure.

All of which adds up to good reasons to look for other opportunities.

# XV

# What's Next?

Will we see leadership from the National Association of Realtors? How I wish! Truly I do. And not necessarily following the path I've laid out here. Something or someone needs to encourage the public to be meaningfully engaged and educated in their real estate dealings. But because the NAR's instruction is primarily directed toward the association's membership and the government, it's unlikely that the public will directly benefit.

Obviously, as I've mentioned, the public is well served by the monitoring of both the ethics of the real estate profession and the government's dealings regarding private property rights. But some needs remain unmet, including the public's need for a higher level of real estate market knowledge. With increased access to real estate ralated information and encouragement to explore and participate in the real estate market, comes a more responsible public. Better educated real estate market participants are less susceptible to downturns in the real estate market. For instance, homeowners can learn to recognize the lifestyle and financial choices that can lead to successful real estate endeavors. Ultimately, greater access to real estate market information and encouragement to take

J. Michael Nolen Jr.

personal responsibility for personal real estate decisions is the unmet need.

The NAR was founded to represent the interests of the real estate profession; one would hope that those interests would also coincide with those of the public. Certainly, in the past the public has greatly benefited. Today though, there is some doubt about that.

Within the ranks of the NAR, there is bickering and debate as to just what its role is in today's world, and what it should have been before the real estate market bust.

Steve Brown, 2014 NAR president, spoke of complaints from small real estate companies about large ones and brokers about their associates, as well as regarding subjects like new technology issues, the slowness of NAR to act, and so on. He responded, "I've heard [their] criticisms...I've witnessed an organization that strives daily to address member needs. During the Great Recession and its aftermath, for example, NAR staff didn't pretend everything was OK. They created the Right Tools, Right Now program, which offered free and discounted business tools to help Realtors carry on during a very challenging time. Have the interests of every member been addressed over time? No. Over the past few years, brokers' needs have sometimes taken a backseat in the association's programming, not because brokers are unimportant, but because NAR has been applying a broad brush to help all members improve their sales."

Sure, with the collapse of the real estate market, there was a need for some additional training of real estate professionals. But that's been how long now? And is that the best use of NAR funds? Rather, might they do that which cannot easily be done by others?

NAR is on the national stage. Their political action committee commands lots of respect. NAR should protect the institution of private property rights at all cost by educating politicians and real estate professionals; then, when a problem as foreboding as the Great Recession is on the horizon, that education should reach directly to the public.

What does it mean, the NAR "didn't pretend everything was OK"? What about the prospective investigative work and the raising of the red flag, accompanied by alarms, that should have occurred long before the bust?

Mr. Brown continues with his "We've Heard You and We Get It" comments: "Here's a sampling of initiatives we've instituted to target many of the frustrations: (a) Committee and forum realignment...(b) Broker Summit...(c) Environmental Summit...to learn from policy experts about the implications of climate change and other environmental issues for the real estate industry."

Notably, he makes no mention of public education, alliances with other large organizations, or direct assistance for homeowners. He also fails to mention systemic economic or real estate industry problems and certainly no attempts at reinventing the real estate industry, much less its own organization.

Now I ask you, regardless of whether you agree with me concerning how best to address the issues of the day: Do you think NAR gets it? By the way, Mr. Brown's comments were made in a particular issue of the *Realtor*® magazine titled, "Keep Calm and Reinvent." Ironic?

Right before the eyes of NAR leadership, and not so subtly, their view of the real estate ecosystem has been shattered, and they don't even realize it. NAR is traveling down Route 66, while the world flies by on the superhighway.

If true leadership is to come from within the real estate industry, apparently it will come from rank-and-file companies and agents, using the resources available to them to improve the public's understanding of real estate. It's a slow and disjointed process, but it's ongoing, and as technology improves, the process will speed up. Strategic alliances will also speed it up—alliances among like-minded professionals within the real estate industry, as well as across a broad spectrum of professionals who work in different but related fields, all with the same goal: providing leadership and order, as I've explained it in this publication.

Personally, I think the Realty Highway process needs to get started quickly and in a big way—in a way that only sizable companies (the Googles, Facebooks, and Zillows of the world) can accomplish. Still, many real estate and financial professionals will press forward, teaching and organizing all facets of the real estate industry.

Until some semblance of order is arrived at, however, the public must be truly engaged in the real estate process, seeking out both micro and macro information from whatever sources are available, latching onto real estate agents who double as teachers schooled in today's issues. Every homeowner, whether his or her property is for sale of not, should have a quality real estate agent, pinpointing a beginning property value estimate, and then offering an annual update of the real estate market. Such agents should also set up automated searches, with alerts of sales activity within the immediate marketplace, representing not only sales activity but also present housing supply. The News Funnel or similar data sources should be sourced for pertinent news, and for firsthand knowledge of the local and national real estate market.

Instead of homeowners asking real estate professionals about the real estate market, real estate professionals should be asking homeowners how their real estate portfolios are. Like a bank statement that is updated regularly (monthly or quarterly), a real estate statement, estimating equity (or at least gross value) as well as projections, should be in the hands of real estate owners. For owner-occupied housing, it should include the estimated cost of alternative shelter. For both owner-occupied housing and investment real estate, it should include an estimate of both retail and wholesale values.

Armed with this type of information, the real estate owner can reply confidently to real estate professionals about his or her personal portfolio. Perhaps technology is not readily available to automate such information completely today. Still, it surely can be approached, and it should be considered in organizing of one's real estate portfolio.

Don't think these are treacherous times? It's a global market, where debt runs rampant among the economies of countries and into the lives of individuals. Though housing prices have increased since the great downturn, the dynamics of the real estate market have changed very little. Real estate values are still at risk. We should allow the pain of the recession, still felt by many, to be the impetus for fundamental change in the way the real estate market operates. We should use twenty-first century thinking to protect the equity of this precious asset—real estate.

# Resources

Altos Research. "About Altos Research." *Altos Research Partners.* October 2014. http://www.altosresearch.com/altos/website/aboutus/partners/.

Altos Research. "Altos Research—How's the Market?" *Altos Research How's the Market RSS.* October 2014. http://blog.altosresearch.com/.

Altos Research. "Oh, You're in Real Estate? How's the Market?" *Altos Research Real Estate Professionals Comments.* October 2014. http://www.altosresearch.com/altos/solutions/realestateprofessionals/.

Barringer, Tory. "Millennials Continue to Delay First Home Purchases." *DS News: The Homepage of the Servicing Industry.* DS News, August 2, 2014 0, 2014. http://dsnews.com/news/08-02-2014/millennials-continue-delay-first-home-purchases.

Blair, Bryce. "Taking Stock: REITs at 50: The Evolution of an Industry." December 2014. Print.

Brown, Steve. "We've Heard You and We Get It." *Realtor.* September–October 2014: 5. Print.

Ceballos, John. "Polk Leads US in Underwater Homes." *The Ledger.* May 8, 2015. Print.

Colwell, Peter F., and Joseph W. Trefzger. "The Economics of Real Estate Principles." Letter. N.d. University of California at Santa Cruz, Santa Cruz, California.

CoreLogic. "CoreLogic Equity Report Fourth Quarter 2013." *CoreLogic Equity Report Fourth Quarter 2013* (2013): n.p. *CoreLogic.* CoreLogic, October 1, 2014. http://www.corelogic.com/research/negative-equity/corelogic-q4-2013-equity-report.pdf

CoreLogic. "CoreLogic National Foreclosure Report April 2014." *CoreLogic National Foreclosure Report April 2014* (2014): n.p. *CoreLogic National Foreclosure Report.* CoreLogic, October 1, 2014. http://www.corelogic.com/research/foreclosure-report/national-foreclosure-report-april-2014.pdf.

CoreLogic. "Our Company." 2014. Web. October 2014. http://www.corelogic.com/downloadable-docs/corelogic-our-company-07-2014.pdf.

*Direct Mortgage Lenders.* New American Funding, October 2014. http://www.newamericanfunding.com/.

Domhoff, G. William. "Who Rules America? Power, Politics, & Social Change. *"Who Rules America? Power, Politics, & Social Change.* University of California at Santa Cruz. October 2014. http://www2.ucsc.edu/whorulesamerica/. Federal Reserve Bank of New York, Student Loan Debt Analysis, 2012, 2013.

Dymi, Amilda. "Millennials, Unaffordability to Drive Homeownership Lower: Zillow." *National Mortgage News*, August 4, 2014. October 20, 2014. http://www.nationalmortgagenews.com/news/origination/millennials-unaffordability-to-drive-homeownership-lower-zillow-1042271-1.html.

"Faceted Classification." *Wikipedia*. Wikimedia Foundation, n.d. October 2014. en.wikipedia.org/wiki/Faceted_classification.

Florida Realtors. "US Homes Lost to Foreclosure Up 25%."*FloridaRealtors.org News*. Florida Realtors®, The Voice for Real Estate in Florida®, September 16, 2010. Web. 2014. floridarealtors.org/NewsAndEvents/article.cfm?id=247023.

Florida Realtors. "Corporations Scoop Up Rental Homes."*FloridaRealtors.org News*. Florida Realtors®, The Voice for Real Estate in Florida®, 2014. Web. October 20, 2014. www.floridarealtors.org/NewsAndEvents/article.cfm?p=1&id=311610.

Fogarty, Mark. "Why Today's Mortgage Market May Be Worse Than After the Collapse." *National Mortgage News*, May 19, 2014. Web. October 20, 2014. http://www.nationalmortgagenews.com/blogs/hearing/why-todays-mortgage-market-may-be-worse-than-after-the-collapse-1041805-1.html.

"HomeZada." *Manage Your Digital Home*. N.d. May 2015. http://www.homezada.com/homeowners.

"How to Buy a House: 21 Steps (with Pictures)." *WikiHow: How to Do Anything.* WikiHow, 2014. Web. October 2014. WikiHow, www.wikihow.com/Buy-a-House#Finalizing_the_Deal_sub.

H.R. Rep. No. 94 (2008). Print.

H.R. Rep. No. 95 (2009). Print.

H.R. Rep. No. 96 (2010). Print.

H.R. Rep. No. 97 (2011). Print.

H.R. Rep. No. 98 (2012). Print.

H.R. Rep. No. 99 (2013). Print.

Keenan, Charles. "REIT Governance: The Capital of Transparency." *Reit.* Reit News, May 19, 2014. Web. Oct. 2014. http://www.reit.com/news/reit-magazine/may-june-2014/reit-governance-capital-transparency.

"About Risk Solutions." *About LexisNexis Risk Solutions.* LexisNexis, 2014. Web. October 2014. http://www.lexisnexis.com/risk/about/.

"MFRMLS Rules & Regulations." *MFRMLS Rules & Regulations.* MFRMLS, June 1, 2006. Web. October 2014. mfrmls.myismart.com/#200.

Morgan, Scott. "High Negative Equity Among Gen-Xers Causing Housing Gridlock." *DS News: The Homepage of the Servicing Industry,* August 26, 2014. Web. October 20, 2014.

https://dsnews.com/news/08-26-2014/high-negative-equity-among-gen-xers-causing-housing-gridlock.

Morgan, Scott. "High Rents Prevent Potential Buyers from Owning Homes." *DS News: The Homepage of the Servicing Industry*, August 22, 2014. Web. October 20, 2014. http://dsnews.com/news/08-22-2014/high-rents-prevent-potential-buyers-owning-homes.

"Onboard Informatics." *Retechnology*. N.p., n.d. Web. October 2014. http://retechnology.com/companies/onboard-informatics/lifestyle-search-engine.

"RealtyTrac: Home Prices Up 13% Due to High-End Sales." *Florida Realtors*, June 24, 2014. Web. October 2014. http://www.floridarealtors.org/NewsAndEvents/article.cfm?id=309986.

Sarasota Realtors. "The Face of Foreclosure Florida." *July* 1, 2009. Web. October 2014. http://www.sarasotarealtors.com/files/hottopics/FaceofForeclosure10040792255.pdf.

"The Code of Ethics." *Realtor.org*. National Association of Realtors, January 1, 2014. Web. October 20, 2014.

"The News Funnel Acquires the CRE App Review." *The News Funnel*, August 4, 2014. Web. October 2014. http://www.thenewsfunnel.com/pressrelease/news-funnel-acquires-cre-app-review.

Thiel, Peter. "Competition Is for Losers." *The Wall Street Journal*. September 12, 2014. Web. October 2014. http://

online.wsj.com/articles/peter-thiel-competition-is-for-losers-1410535536.

Timiraos, Nick. "How Weak Is Housing? Five Charts Tell the Story." *The Wall Street Journal* (2014): n.p. Web. August 7, 2014. http://blogs.wsj.com/economics/2014/08/07/how-weak-is-housing-five-charts-tell-the-story/.

Timiraos, Nick, Jessica Silver-Greenburg, and Dan Fitzpatrick. "Mortgage Damage Spreads." *The Wall Street Journal* (2010): n.p. Web. 2014.

Jean Harris Nolen Foster, Jo Nolen Fleming; Tapestry, 2005.

"Title Search." *Wikipedia.* Wikimedia Foundation, n.d. Web. October 2014. Wikipedia.org/wiki/Title.search.

Trendgraphix. "Trendgraphix Facts Trend." *Trendgraphix*, June 21, 2014. Web. http://myreport.trendgraphix.com/.

Trendgraphix. "Facts Trends." *Trendgraphix*, Web. October 20, 2014. http://trendgraphix.com/.

Tuman, Diane. "For Sale by Owner: Flat Fee MLS Services." *Zillow*, n.d. Web. October 2014. http://www.zillow.com/wikipages/For-Sale-By-Owner-Flat-Fee-MLS-Services/.

Weintraub, Elizabeth. "Home Buying and Selling: How to Buy or Sell a Home." *About Home Buying.* N.p., 2014. Web. October 2014. http://homebuying.about.com/od/buyingahome/qt/0307Buyinghome.htm. Closing Process, homeclosoing101.org/closing.cfm.

Weise, Karen. "Does Better Real Estate Data Encourage Racial Segregation?" *Bloomberg Business Week.* May 1, 2014. Web. Oct. 2014. http://www.businessweek.com/articles/2014-05-01/does-better-real estate-data-encourage-racial-segregation.

Weisenthal, Joe. "The Analyst Who Nailed the Housing Crash Is Quietly Revealing the Next Big Thing." Business Insider, Aug. 10, 2014.

Wells Fargo. "Wells Fargo Survey Reveals Consumer Views on Homebuying." *Wells Fargo,* September 15, 2014. Web. October 20, 2014. https://www.wellsfargo.com/about/press/2014/consumer-views-homebuying_0915.

Yun, Lawrence. "Realtors Confidence Index Report on the May 2014 Survey." N.d., n.p. *Realtor.* National Association of Realtors, 4 Jun. 2014. Web. 2014. http://www.realtor.org/sites/default/files/reports/2014/2014-05-realtors-confidence-index-06-23-2014.pdf.

Zillow. "Zillow Real Estate Market Report August 2014." *Real Estate Market Report.* Aug. 2014: N.p. Sep. 2014. Web. Oct. 2014. http://cdn2.blog-media.zillowstatic.com/3/2014_AugustReport_Zillow_a_02-ec5bbf.pdf.

www.ingramcontent.com/pod-product-compliance
Lightning Source LLC
Chambersburg PA
CBHW071806170526
45167CB00003B/1190